Northern Colorado Ghost Stories

*True Ghost Stories from Estes Park, Fort Collins, Glen Haven,
Livermore, Longmont, and Loveland*

Nancy Hansford

Nancy Hansford (signature)

Indian Hills BookWorks

PUBLISHED BY
Indian Hills BookWorks
1900 Mohawk Street
Fort Collins, CO 80525

Library of Congress Control Number: 2005907683

Printed and bound in the United States of America.

First printing, September 2005
Second printing, October 2005
Third printing, October 2006

Editing: Pam Fellers
Layout and Design: Odyssey Publications
Indexer: Odyssey Publications

For those who believe, no explanation is necessary and for those who don't, no explanation is possible.

Table of Contents

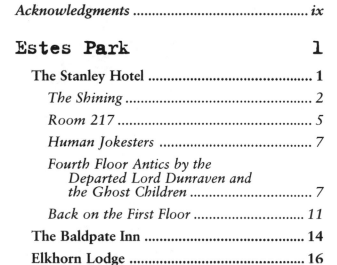

Fort Collins 65

Acknowledgments

It is a privilege to acknowledge the contributions and support of the following people: my husband, Bruce and all of my family and friends.

The following talented people have made this book a quality product:

Compiler and Layout Designer, Elizabeth Hansford

Book Cover Designer, Dick Greenberg

Map Designer, Brian Sullivan

Editor, Pam Fellers

Thank you to everyone who willingly shared his or her stories with me. This project would have been more challenging without the many leads provided by so many.

The helpful librarians of the Estes Park, Longmont, Loveland, and Fort Collins Libraries made my job of checking historical facts much easier.

I appreciate the tutoring and sharing from all of the intuitives and paranormal investigators who allowed me to enter their worlds.

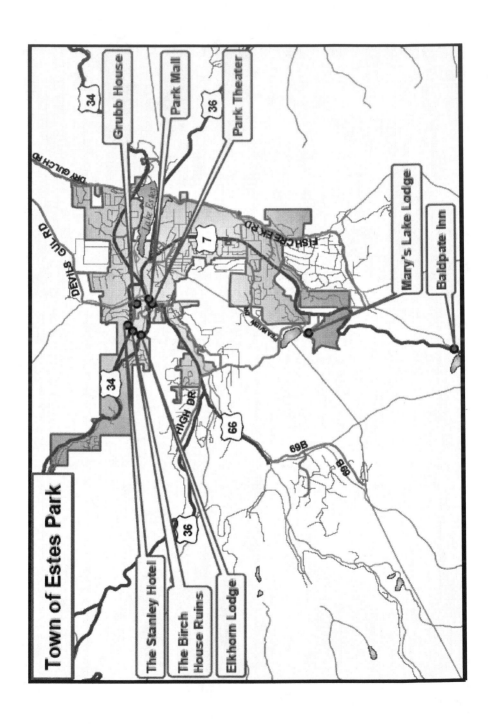

Estes Park

This beautiful mountain town of Estes Park is renowned for the beauty of the powerful Rocky Mountains surrounding it. The beauty and the wild history all add to the infamous ghost stories running rampant in the village.

The Stanley Hotel

The Stanley Hotel is the eye catching, huge white structure holding court from the southern hilltop above Estes Park village. This old hotel was built in the early 1900's by F.O. Stanley, who created the Stanley Steam Engine, a steam powered horseless carriage. This Georgian style hotel opened in 1909 and looks like it should stand on the east coast. Thanks to F.O. and his vision, it belongs to Colorado—and Oh! What secrets it holds within its walls.

Often called the most haunted place in Colorado; the Stanley Hotel is host to more spooky characters than human ones. Phantom children run up and down hallways and the great Steinway piano unexpectedly plays into the night by itself. F.O. Stanley, the genius builder of the hotel still keeps an eye on the place. Lord Dunraven, a wealthy scoundrel and ladies man, never outgrew his desire for the ladies on the fourth floor—even after passing to the other side.

Several mediums and psychics have reported they dislike being in the hotel because the energy from the paranormal activity is overwhelming, coming down around them like a firestorm. However, it is agreed that the known spirits arc definitely curious and mischievous, but not dangerous in any way.

The Shining

Stephen King was inspired to write the *Shining* when he visited the Stanley with his wife on closing day in October, 1972. King asked the clerk if he and his wife could have a room. The clerk told him yes, but there was only one American Express sales form left. Coincidentally, American Express was the only card King had with him. King jokes that *The Shining* wouldn't have been written if there were no more sales forms. That was an amazing coincidence. Did one of the hotel ghosts save that credit card form just for King?

F.O. Stanley, genius inventor, built the hotel for his wife and friends who wanted to enjoy the finer things in the west.

The original *Shining* movie by Stanley Kubrick was not filmed at the Stanley. Producer Kubrick scouted out the Stanley for the setting and didn't like anything he saw. He said it wasn't isolated and there wasn't enough snow, etc. etc. So he shot the majority of the movie on a London Sound Stage and used the Timberline Lodge in the Mt. Hood, Oregon area for the outside shots.

Stephen King returned to the Stanley in 1995 to film the *Shining* TV miniseries on the site where he wrote the novel and originally stayed in Room 217. No one knows what King experienced while staying in the infamous room. When King returned to the Stanley for the miniseries filming, there were not any paranormal events but the whole project was great fun for locals.

A Fort Collins couple, Joel and Betty Husted, participated in the miniseries filming with their 1941 Cadillac. Betty's late husband, Joel was mainly involved in the scenes, repeatedly driving his car up to the hotel during an afternoon of filming. Betty reports she did not meet up with any of the spirits while they were on site. In fact, Betty worked at the Stanley Gift Shop in the summer of 1942 and didn't see any spirits then.

According to Paula Peat Page Martin, King referred to the former hotel manager, who in real life was Frank Normali, in his book as an "officious prick." While visiting the miniseries set, Normali asked the author for an autograph and wanted to

The Stanley Hotel is a focal point of the Estes Valley.

be sure to have it addressed to "that officious prick." Stephen King obliged.

When Martin was sales and marketing director for the hotel, she organized the details for the *Shining* miniseries film crew. She does not believe in ghosts. She still says that even after her experience...

The Stanley hotel management and the film company agreed to honor the schedules of all guests who were staying at the hotel during the filming. One evening, a local chapter of the American Association of University Women had scheduled a buffet and awards ceremony for 7 p.m. The crew was to stop filming by 5 p.m. in order to give the staff time to set up the event. The producer came to Martin and told her they were having such a good time filming in the Billiards Room that they wanted to continue until 6 p.m., promising they would help with the set up for the program afterwards. Martin agreed.

To create the creepy effect needed for the movie shoot, the lobby had been cleared of all of its traditional furniture and replaced with over-sized, sometimes grotesquely exaggerated, pieces such as a table with animal legs and claw feet. Martin was working with the staff in the lobby and told the catering director she was going to the storage room for tablecloths to cover the movie set tables.

She headed for the storage room. Suddenly Paula felt like she was alone in a very quiet, unoccupied lobby until she heard a voice behind her calling her name. She turned around and saw no one. In fact, she didn't see anyone else in the huge lobby. She continued to the storage room and heard her name called again, but still, no one was there.

Martin gathered the tablecloths and returned to the bustling lobby. She asked if the catering director had left the lobby and who was calling her (Martin's) name. The catering director said, "Paula, I've been here the whole time and so has everyone else. I didn't see anyone following you or hear anyone calling your name. People have been here helping us set up the entire time you were gone."

Martin explains the whole incident as a very weird experience. She doesn't know what happened except that she knows it did happen. But remember, she doesn't believe in ghosts.

Room 217

The story behind incidents in Room 217 began in the early years when the hotel rooms were heated by gas lamps and a horrible accident occurred when one of the maids entered the room to light the lamp. She turned on the gas lamp and realized she had no matches with her, so she left to retrieve some, leaving the gas lamp valve open. Upon returning, she lit a match, and the accumulated gas exploded, driving her through the floor to

Room 217 is the infamous Stephen King room. What did he see while staying there?

the dining room below. She broke both legs and suffered other injuries. F.O. Stanley, a very generous employer, covered all of her medical bills during her long recovery. He kept her job for her and even gave her a raise and a promotion when she resumed working. The loyal maid stayed and worked at the Stanley for many more years.

She even carried her loyalty into the afterlife by continuing to care for guests of Room 217.

This story about the maid seemed doubtful until recently, when research in the Estes Park Library revealed a 1974 oral history interview by this author with longtime resident, Bertha Ramey. During that interview, she reported the maid's story as told to her by Charles Hix, another longtime Estes resident who had first hand knowledge of the maid and F.O. Stanley.

Recent guests recount that after checking into 217, they tossed their bags on the bed and left to enjoy some sightseeing. Upon returning, their bags were unpacked and their clothing neatly put away.

Another untidy guest said he went to sleep in Room 217 with his clothes tossed all around. He woke up the next morning to find them folded and placed in drawers and his shoes neatly lined up in a row.

F.O. Stanley probably had no idea of the extent of the loyalty his maid would demonstrate for his thoughtfulness. Loyalty far beyond...

Actor Jim Carrey stayed in Room 217 for only one night while filming *Dumb and Dumber*. He left the hotel hurriedly the next morning saying he would never stay there again, but refused to reveal what he saw.

Human Jokesters

The Stanley Tour Director, Billy tells of the elderly couple from Fort Collins, Colorado who visits the hotel frequently and always reserves Room 217.

The couple stays up late into the night. When the couple hears hotel guests approaching, they open the door to the hallway slowly. He makes a frightening noise and the wife does her part by calling out in a spooky voice. They take great delight in watching the visitors running away from the door as fast as they can.

The morning after, the couple always reports to the registration desk about how many unsuspecting ghost hunters "They scared last night."

Fourth Floor Antics by the Departed Lord Dunraven and the Ghost Children

F.O. Stanley purchased the land for the Stanley Hotel from Lord Dunraven, a foreigner who took advantage of a law that stated only American citizens could purchase land. Dunraven sought out a number of seedy characters and offered them a pittance to purchase land on his behalf. Next, he paid them another small amount to sign the land over to him. When his scheme was discovered, he was run out of town.

➤ ⫯ ⫯ ⫷

When the Stanley Hotel opened, it catered to the very wealthy of the day. The guests arrived at the hotel with nannies to care for their children. The unfortunate nannies were stashed up on the stuffy fourth floor, which was actually the hotel attic where large dormitory-like rooms were filled with cots separated only by cloth dividers to provide a small bit of privacy for the servants. The nannies always had to care for their young charges on the fourth floor, because children were not allowed to run throughout the hotel.

Today, many guests have complained to the staff about the noisy children running up and down the fourth floor hallways throughout the night and keeping them awake. In each case, the registration clerks have verified there were no children staying on the fourth floor.

Other guests have claimed to see a little girl running up and down the hallway and then disappearing. The Tour Guide, Billy, says the fourth floor hallways make him feel very uneasy. Are the little ghosts seeking their revenge for not being allowed to play anywhere else in the hotel?

If you really want to sight a spirit, you should sit on the small couch on the fourth floor. That seems to be the best spot for

ghost sighting as recommended by Billy. Recently, a group of teenage girls celebrated a birthday with an overnight party there and spent the night on that couch waiting for ghostly appearances while comforting themselves with cookies and milk. We don't know what they experienced.

Madame Vera, an Estes Park medium, said she has seen the children playing with a ball in the fourth floor hallway. She has

The dignified portrait of the historical scandalous villain, Lord Dunraven belies his shady business deals and romps with the ladies.

also smelled a hint of cigar smoke in one corner of the Billiards Room.

Lord Dunraven is still spotted on the fourth floor often. During his mortal years, he spent a lot of time there because he enjoyed charming the nannies. It is reported that he owned a brothel in England before making the journey to Estes Park. Sometimes you can see him or "someone" dressed in clothing of the late 19th century peering out of the window of Room 407.

One of the most active rooms is 418 where maids will not enter alone as they say "someone" grabs them when they enter. Lord Dunraven did love the ladies... However, staff members will tell you Room 401 has more ghostly activity than 418. In fact, the spookiness in Room 401 might make believers out of almost anyone.

Karen Lynch, former sales and marketing director will tell you she does not believe in ghosts even though she has experienced several events.

The Stanley Hotel ghost children play ball in the fourth floor hallway and sometimes disturb guests with their gleeful running back and forth...

One day, Lynch was working on the reservation desk when Rev. Kimberly Henry called to make reservations for the summer solstice, June 21. Henry is also a psychic and requested that she and her husband be given a room on the fourth floor. Lynch obliged and reserved Room 401 for them.

When Henry and her husband arrived, Lynch was unable to meet them. During their stay of several days, Kimberly Henry never came down from her room saying she did not feel well. Lynch offered her the standard advice for overcoming altitude sickness by suggesting Henry drink three times more fluids than she would at lower altitudes.

Altitude sickness was not Henry's problem.

When she finally left her room to meet Lynch in the lobby, Lynch came out from behind the registration desk to greet her. Henry was facing the Lord Dunraven portrait at the west end of the lobby. When she spotted it, she said, "Oh my God" and dropped to her knees sobbing. She said, "He is the man who has been in my room all this time. He has stood at the foot of my bed and appeared in the corner of the room."

Later on back in their room, Kimberly Henry's husband removed his wedding ring and placed it on the bathroom sink. Suddenly, it was thrown without human help into the drain and his eyeglasses were thrown off a table.

Everyone thought Lord Dunraven was acting up and dropped the ring into the drain to show his displeasure for the husband. Lord Dunraven is keeping his reputation of loving the ladies alive though, isn't he.

Early in her stay, Rev. Henry also complained of smelling cigar smoke but Lynch reminded her that 401 is a non smoking room. Later in the week, Henry told Lynch, Lord Dunraven had appeared to her standing by the closet smoking a cigar.

Back on the First Floor

The most often told story is the tale surrounding the Steinway piano displayed in its own alcove in the Music Room on the east end of the first floor. The Steinway was a gift from F.O. to his wife Flora. It was hauled in pieces up the canyon then reassembled to live in the hotel. Flora has been heard by many employees and guests playing her beloved piano. She always stops the moment someone crosses the threshold of the entry. A few say they have seen a shadowy presence seated at the keyboard and others say they thought they were seeing a player piano because the keys were moving by themselves. The great Steinway is not a player piano.

F.O. Stanley still oversees his hotel, but is better behaved than Lord Dunraven. A number of hotel clerks have reported looking up from working at the registration desk and seeing F.O.'s tall presence for a brief moment. Hotel bartenders have also reported F.O. Stanley's fleeting presence dressed in a black jacket standing at their bar.

Flora Stanley loved her Steinway piano when she was alive. Some say she still plays it, but she doesn't like an audience.

A hotel housekeeper named Leslie Dawson has reported being locked in rooms endlessly. Marty Yochum Casey has spoken of seeing, not hearing Flora Stanley at her piano. Casey was at a hotel reunion gathering at the Stanley Museum when she related this story to a reporter from the *Estes Park Trail Gazette*. Mark Lorenz was formerly employed in the hotel engineering department and explained a little known tunnel running from the hotel to staff quarters was reopened in 1983. The tunnel had apparently been closed off for some time. Employees use it to pass to the next building without going outside.

There aren't any reports of paranormal activity in the tunnel—yet.

One of the most heartfelt stories is about a woman and her husband who honeymooned at the hotel before he went off to World War II. He told her that he had never been as happy as when they were at the Stanley, and he would see her there again. He did not return from duty, but some time after his death, the grieving widow did return and reunited with him in another way.

F.O. Stanley appears briefly at the registration desk to keep the clerks on their toes.

She was seen often, wandering the halls talking to someone who was not visible to anyone else and appeared to be very content.

The widow soon moved to Estes Park and spent a great deal of time at the Stanley—where she was observed visiting with her beloved husband.

The Stanley stairwell is a hot spot and collecting point for active spiritual energy.

The Bridal Room and private balcony are very comfortable for newlyweds unless Lord Dunraven acts up.

The Baldpate Inn

*When Gordon Mace decided to build the inn, he and his wife Ethel were visited by Earl Biggers who wrote the book, **Seven Keys to Baldpate**, he also authored the Charlie Chan mysteries.*

Biggers spent the night with the Maces in their homestead cabin and told the Maces about his book which is about a hotel only open in the summer. It was seven miles out of the city and closed in the winter. Thus the inn was named Baldpate. Biggers sent them a key which he called the original key to Baldpate.

Travel the narrow dirt road to the Inn and before you know it, the massive log structure looms on your right. Everything here is oversized except the resident spirit; she is gentle and minds her own business—most of the time.

There is so much energy from the keys circulating around the Inn, and all of it is accom-panied by Ethel Mace's ghostly figure

Thousands of keys, from all over the globe, displayed in the famous Baldpate Inn Key Room.

keeping vigil from her rocker and appearing to be reading her bible. Ethel reputedly doesn't like smokers in her Baldpate either. Ask any smoking guests if they have trouble keeping lit up, especially when she is watching.

Ethel's spirit sits in a rocking chair surrounded by her key collection. The collection includes keys from Hitler's desk, Westminster Abbey (stolen by a college student), the key of life taken from King Tut's neck when they opened his tomb (donated by one of the presiding scientists), and the first key in the collection, which was donated by Clarence Darrow, the infamous Chicago lawyer.

The picturesque sign of seven wooden keys outside the historic Baldpate was handmade by Gordon Mace Sr. who was a patternmaker.

Baldpate Inn's Ethel Mace sits in her rocking chair surrounded by her key collection and reading the Bible.

Elkhorn Lodge

*When you enter the Elkhorn Lodge property, it seems
friendly enough. The staff and owner are very
accommodating. As you walk into the cavernous, dark lobby
area, the energy from the many years and hundreds of guests
hangs over everything, seeping out of the walls.*

*Stand quietly for a moment and you will swear you're not
alone and you're probably not. Those accompanying you are
not easily seen, however. Just be patient... They don't want to
hurt anyone. Not Really. Except for the time they set the
fire. That was a ghostly stunt that almost went too far.*

Sam Hackett was an employee at the lodge and recently described
his paranormal experiences while there. The Elkhorn was built
in 1874 and President Teddy Roosevelt used to stay there often.
Hackett painted a portrait of him that has been hanging in the
dining room.

One day Hackett was taking pictures of the teepees located
behind the bunkhouses. He took a photo of the largest teepee
with an instamatic camera and when the film was developed,
there was a huge man standing in front of the teepee. The teepee
was visible through the transparent figure.

Hackett showed the photo to an Elkhorn wrangler, Dawn
who confirmed she could also see the figure who was wearing old
western clothing with a leather vest and holding a whip. She
told Hackett the figure was the well known stagecoach driver
who used to pick people up in Denver and bring them to the
Elkhorn in the old days. Everyone was afraid of him because
he was so big and so mean. Dawn verified what Hackett
photographed. However, she couldn't tell him why the image
was fading from the photograph...

Dawn also told Hackett the Lodge is believed to be haunted by Eleanor James, the daughter of the man who built it, William James. Other employees who worked in housekeeping said they could not move the rocking chair in Eleanor's room. If they did, things would begin to fly through the air.

Eleanor married Peter Hondius, a European who first visited the lodge as a guest. She and her husband managed the Elkhorn properties for many years. She was responsible for the lodge and he lived in the national park, dealing with their interests there. Eleanor spent her life managing the lodge and later wrote a journal about her lifetime there. We could not find any copies of the journal but if we had, would it have explained why many say she still controls Room 7 where she lived?

Jerry Zahourek has owned the Elkhorn since 1990. When he opened in the fall of 1991, he threw a party for 50-60 people. During the party, two of the guests, a clerk of the court in Estes and her daughter, went to their room to rest. They returned later and reported that someone blowing in their hair awakened them from their naps. They could feel his presence, but not see him...or her.

The historic Elkhorn Lodge holds many surprises for visitors. If only the walls could talk...

Zahourek has not seen first hand what his guests have witnessed, but related one of his own experiences: About the turn of the millennium, a wedding party booked reservations in August for their celebration. They went to bed very late on the night of the wedding.

The next morning Zahourek awakened early and fixed coffee, after which he walked around the lodge to check on everything. He was alone as everyone else was still asleep. He walked through the dining room and everything was all right. The movable gas stove he had used for the event was still in the dining room where he left it the night before. There was nothing else around it and certainly nothing sitting on it. The pilot light was not on.

Soon he began to smell something burning, he thought at first it might be the worn wiring in the old lodge. Suddenly, a small fire broke out, and it was discovered coming from the gas stove with the pilot light still turned off and rubber mats that had not been there earlier when Zahourek was making his rounds to check on things, were now sitting on top of the stove. The overheated rubber mats turned out to be the source of the fire. The smell of the burning rubber led him to the stove.

There was no one else up at that hour. Zahourek was alone the entire time.

Zahourek did not believe in ghosts as he had not seen any, but he believed others who told him they had seen them. He feels the fire was a prank by the resident spirits.

Many other guests in recent years have reported figures appearing in their rooms or the hallways and fading into the walls. Zahourek said he believes all of their stories because they were all credible people, although he has not witnessed the vanishing ghost figures personally. What are the secrets the Elkhorn ghosts and apparitions have kept all these years?

Mary's Lake Lodge

When you drive south on Hwy. 7 from Estes Park for six miles, you will spot the large log and stone Mary's Lake Lodge nestled high on the eastern slope of the Rocky Mountains at the base of Rams Horn Mountain. It almost seems to take over the mountain with its size. The darkness of the lodge against the green of the mountain makes it appear mysterious and haunted. Once inside the friendly lobby, you won't feel like it's mysterious any longer. However, haunted is another matter...

The Mary's Lake Lodge ghosts are both shy and very protective of their lodge.

One recent snowy night at 11:30 p.m., a lone employee was walking by herself to her car which was parked behind the lodge. There was no one else around. As she approached her car she saw an older gentleman, wearing a plaid suit jacket, standing by the building. He didn't speak to her, just stood watching as she entered her car.

As she backed the car up and drove off, she looked for him, but he had disappeared. She saw no footprints in the snow where he was standing or would have left them, if he had actually walked away in the earthly sense.

Rene' Schiaffo, the restaurant manager was closing one night by herself. She went upstairs, closed all doors to all the rooms and shut off all the lights. When she finished and was heading downstairs, she was very shocked to see all of her work undone. All the doors were reopened, and all of the lights were turned on again. Schiaffo left hurriedly, leaving the lights on and the doors opened just as the ghostly residents wanted them to be.

On July 6, 1978, fire broke out in the south wing which housed the employees. The exact cause remains a mystery, although some say it was an electrical malfunction. Look at the photographs on the mantle in the dining room and check out the photograph of the dramatic blaze which holds a ghostly secret for the very observant...

After the fire, the main lodge was condemned and remained closed for ten years. There were a few intermittent openings and closings during that time. The old lodge waited patiently for the right person, who had the spark and wherewithal to bring it back to life, to come along.

When construction workers were rebuilding Mary's Lake Lodge, they reported many times that their power tools turned on and off by themselves with no human help. The owner of the lodge finally hired a medium to calm the spiritual events down a bit, since employees reported so many experiences. The professional medium moved through all of the rooms to clear the ghostly energies. She reported sensing that a little girl had drowned in one of the bathtubs on the second floor. There

Some say there is a figure of a small girl standing on the railing on the right. There was no actual girl seen there during the fire.

haven't been any documented reports of such a tragedy, so no one could verify it.

Schiaffo grew up in Estes Park. She and her teenage friends found the creepy, abandoned lodge to be a great clandestine party place. One night when the teens sneaked into the abandoned lodge, Schiaffo walked upstairs, taking the rickety stairs from the lobby. The stairs gave way and she fell through the floor into the basement. She was not hurt, just scared out of her wits. Even so, she returned as a loyal employee and has been observing and hearing about unexplainable events since her first day of employment in 2002. She and the other employees will not leave the lodge late at night by themselves anymore. Is there safety in numbers?

The Mary's Lake bartender, Andy, experienced an event similar to Schiaffo's; when closing up alone one night at 2 a.m. He walked through the building and, like Schiaffo had, he turned off all the lights and closed all the doors. He also turned off the music in the bar. Suddenly, the music came on again by itself with the volume turned all the way up, and the lights were turned on by a ghostly someone to show all the doors had been reopened. Andy too, retreated very quickly and left the spirits to their mischief without him.

An Estes Park medium, known as Rosemary the Celtic Lady, held a metaphysical healing seminar for a large group gathered in the lodge. The amazed and emotional audience was given information precious to each of them regarding deceased loved ones. Rosemary stated that she felt more paranormal energy at Mary's Lake Lodge than she had sensed at the Stanley.

The audience was astounded by Rosemary's ability to communicate with and channel the dearly departed. That included the new marketing director, Karen Lynch, formerly of the Stanley. Despite her experiences with a couple of paranormal happenings at the Stanley, Lynch still maintained she did not believe in such things. That is, until Rosemary saw Lynch's deceased mother in the lodge and told Lynch something about her that only someone actually communicating with Mom could know.

The walls of the historic Mary's Lodge hold many stories. But a ghostly old man and a young girl are the most active spirits who remain to watch over the revitalized restoration and mortal activities of human guests. Just don't be surprised if they let you know they're still going to give their opinions now and then.

The Lodge opened in 1913 and has hosted decades of tourists. The memories and events captured in its walls live in the hearts of people from all over the world. In case current visitors forget, there are vigilant spirits standing ready to remind them.

The Birch House

The blackened stone framework visible from the municipal square near the center of town stands silently up on the rocky ridge directly north of Elkhorn Avenue. Those who don't know the story, always ask about the ruins.

The house was owned by Al Birch, a colorful character who had the house built. He lived in it for a short time until it burned down on a cold December night. He worked for the Denver Post for many years and spent the summers in Estes Park with his wife and daughter.

If you stand in the corner of the burned out house, look up at the third star from the left in the southern sky and you might see Al Birch, striding across the night horizon.

The Birch house was one of the first structures built in Estes Park during the early 1900's. It's a credit to the stonemason Carl Piltz that the stone walls outlining the home are still standing strong after being exposed to nearly a century of mountain weather.

Birch lived in his cabin on the hill for a short time until the fire destroyed it. On the night of December 21, 1907, he said, "I was awakened by the house being full of smoke. It's a wonder I ever woke up, because I could barely stagger out of bed and try to locate the source of the smoke."

"I grabbed a pair of overalls, a pair of cowboy boots, a hat and jacket; ran out on my porch and started yelling at the top of my voice for help. There was no fire department in those early days, but men down on the main street heard me and ran up to the house as quickly as they could. It was too late to do any good and the place burned down..."

Birch was relieved he managed to save his treasured cowboy hat because it was a gift from Tom Mix, the silent film star. F.O. Stanley, owner of the Stanley Hotel, often borrowed that hat from his friend to wear to cowboy dances.

A Letter to the Editor of the Trail Gazette in July, 2000 offered another Al Birch story: "It is true the structure of the ruins was never rebuilt; however, it was replaced by the small log cabin along Black Canyon Creek just north of the Municipal Building. Al Birch started it just two weeks after the fire and built the entire structure himself, except for the brick chimney. He and his family spent many summers in the new cabin."

Al Birch died May 10, 1972 at the age of 89, leaving the mysterious landmark on the hilltop. His spiritual energy remains to greet all visitors who walk the path to his summer roost on top of the hill.

Al Birch's spiritual energy waits in the corner by the fireplace to welcome visitors.

The Grubb House

The Grubb House and Forest Service Cabin are located on Virginia Avenue in Estes Park. Frank Grubb was a carpenter working for F.O. Stanley on the Stanley Hotel in 1909 the same year he built his house.

The house is restored with immaculate detail and almost seems to be resting at last recovering from its chaotic past. At least, we think it is peaceful now. Old, violent spirits won't return once they've been sent away, will they?

It is thought the Grubbs may have lost their daughter Marjorie, possibly to a horseback riding accident while living in the house. One of the troublesome ghosts might have been her, along with other lost spirits, who caused the current owners so many disturbances that they resorted to having the place exorcised. The current owner's research into the census from 1920 and 1930 confirmed the daughter's existence. However, since that time there has been no available open record or knowledge of her. The owner acknowledges she may still be alive but feels it is unlikely.

The Grubb House has been completely restored and cleared of its ghostly past.

While the ghosts remained in the home, things often flew off the walls and there were so many other disturbances, the family wondered why they ever moved into the attractive home. At one point, when it seemed a great deal of the activity centered on a spindle rocker, so the owners sold it. As a result, the ghostly activity slowed down a little bit, but did not end.

The family moved out for a couple of days while the paranormal experts completed their work. The home on Virginia Drive is so peaceful now that it is hard to imagine it was once known as the most haunted house in town.

Diligent research by the owner has not turned up any other background on the spirits who were so determined to drive them out of the house. The clearing of the house has worked, the spirits have moved on to wherever banished spirits go.

The Park Theater

This white framed woman stands tall in the Estes Park Village. But her tower is empty, as empty of emotion as the woman she was meant to memorialize. The real story lies within the walls of the theater.

The heartbroken spirit who still lives in the Park Theater is Ralph Gwynn. He bought the theater and built the tower addition in the mid 1920's as a monument to the love of his life after she left him stranded at the altar. The aging beauty of the tower is symbolic of the way Ralph felt about his disappearing lover, beautiful on the outside and empty on the inside. The tower is completely hollow.

J.L. Jackson built the Park Theater in 1913. Ralph Gwynn added the tower in the mid 1920s as a monument to his runaway bride. The tower is beautiful on the outside and empty on the inside—the same as Gwynn's disappearing love.

The current owner, Sharon Seeley knows Ralph's spirit still resides in his theater. One day, when she was working alone in the building, she adjusted the newly installed control board for the projector. She left it for awhile and returned to find every adjustment she had made to be changed drastically. She knew that she was alone in the building and that no one else could have entered the control booth. No one, that is, of the mortal world.

She rents the theater out for weddings and remembers something that happened regarding a wedding held there for a member of her own family. The rehearsal was the night before and afterward, one of the bridesmaids accidentally left her shoes in a particular place in the theater. The shoes were not in that place the next morning and were never found until much later when Seeley was working in the building and found the shoes on an outside ledge where no one would have gone unless they were doing repair work on the theater. Perhaps Ralph's spirit was expressing his frustration with weddings.

The Park Mall

The entrance to the mall is nondescript. From the Elkhorn Street entrance, it appears to be just a mall in a mountain village. But there is more here than meets the eye. If you're lucky, you will see much more than the merchandise and other people crowding the walkway. The mall was the transportation depot for Estes Park in earlier days. Historical spiritual beings lurk about the mall while they try to complete unfinished business or find their lost loved ones.

Madame Vera, a professional medium who consults with clients in the mall, along with some of the mall merchants reported seeing a filmy presence of a woman pass through the mall from time to time. Vera senses the wandering spirit is looking for a lost love.

Robin Pollack, the owner of the Intrigue Shop located in the Mall, believes that an unseen someone, whom she has named Curtis, plays with the doorbell system in her shop during the early hours when she is working there alone. The doorbell has rung from time to time signaling that someone is entering, although no one is. And no, the system does not have an electrical short or any other technical problem.

One of the employees in the Intrigue Shop has experienced a spiritual event of another kind. She lives in an old 1920's vintage house in Estes, which she shares with a very color prejudiced spirit. She cannot keep purple towels in her bathroom. Every time she buys new (purple) towels and hangs them on the rack, the (purple) towels disappear soon after. She really wants purple towels in her bathroom. We say to her, keep trying. Maybe you can outlast them.

The woman's grandson has seen a young boy, dressed in clothes from another time, in the house. He has not been frightened by the phantom child and is the only family member to have witnessed the boy's presence.

There is a small snack shop outside the Park Mall directly across from the theater. One very hot day, Sharon Seeley was working in the corner of the tiny shop. The heat was overwhelming, and there was no air conditioning. Suddenly, she and others in that corner felt a chilling cold. It didn't carry over into the rest of the shop and there was no earthly reason for it. Cold spots often signal the presence of spirits; sort of a ghostly air conditioning system...

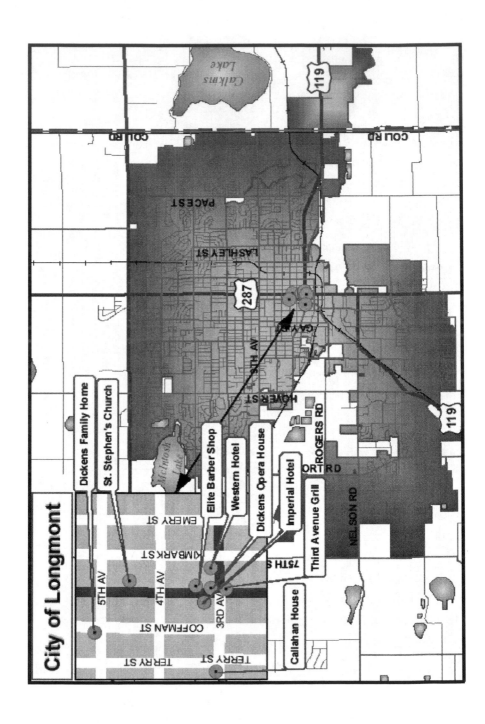

Longmont

Longmont is a normal enough Front Range city with a prevailing pride and concern for the local history and historical structures. Impressive restoration has taken place as awareness of the town's colorful history has grown. However, many of those spirited characters, some great, some questionable, have opted to remain for reasons known only to them.

The Spirit Connection Gift Shop and Dickens Family Mansion

Gail and Eric Jones, who are certified paranormal investigators, own the shop. Gail is also an intuitive.

Eric and Gail, along with Dori Spence—another intuitive—are based in Longmont and have formed an organization of like-minded people who have an interest in researching and understanding the afterlife. The organization is SPOOKS, Society for the preservation of the Ostracization or Obliteration of Kinderd Sprits.

Gail said that when she was searching for a new location for Spirit Connection and she found this house at 307 Coffman, she felt comfortable in it the moment she entered.

The house has presented the couple with enough spiritual activity to make them feel right at home. Eric has heard children giggling in the hallway. Another day, he said that something unseen entered the shop and passed in front of the infrared

The Daughter of W. H. Dickens lived in what is now the Spirit Connection Gift Shop with her husband and mother.

doorbell sensor, setting it off and, shortly afterward, passed by the detector, setting it off again, on his way out. At the time, there was no one in the shop with him except the unseen doorbell ringer.

The large light brick building on the corner of Third and Coffman next door was the original Dickens family mansion. W.H. Dickens was allegedly shot to death by his son, although the son was never convicted of the crime. Shortly after that sordid business, Mrs. Dickens moved next door to the 307 Coffman address to live with her daughter and son-in-law. At that time, the family mansion property on the corner of Third and Coffman was gifted to the city of Longmont to be converted into Longmont's first hospital. The third floor of the mansion accommodated the pediatrics ward.

A hospital cleaning lady told Gail and Eric her own playful spooky story. The cleaning lady said that when she mopped the third floor and the long hallway there, she saw rolls of toilet paper rolling down the corridor. She thought it might be kids playing a prank, but she was the only one there. When the toilet paper incident happened more than once, she decided to try communicating with the vaporous culprit.

She brought a ball to the hospital corridor and rolled it down the hallway, the ball stopped midway and rolled back to her. No one was there returning the ball to her. Eventually, a ghostly boy revealed himself to her and we assume they "played ball" often.

The cleaning lady's employment at the hospital ended before a fire which heavily damaged the third floor, occurred. When she returned some time after the destructive fire to visit the hospital, she reported she had no more sightings of the little boy.

Now, the former Dickens mansion, currently Dickens Manor, is home to transient citizens.

Gail said that, even with the sometimes chaotic activity next door at Dickens Manor, she still feels very protected in their shop by a spiritual presence who looks out for them and keeps everything safe.

Gail said, "It's almost like ghosts find ways to let us know they're around. I don't hear them talk, but there are other ways for them to communicate." Through a series of traumatic events, Gail experienced that for herself...

She said, "When I came out to Colorado, I worked for a company that opened up the Caribou Mine and some other properties. They had recovered some old things from the mines and among them there was a box of rusty old horseshoes. I brought one of the horseshoes home and gave it to my son, Michael to hang above his bedroom door for luck."

"When Michael was in high school, he worked for a gas station and he signed up with the Marlboro sales rep to receive advertising stuff in the mail. He received crazy items from them all the time."

"Then, our son was killed by a drunk driver. About a month after the funeral, a little square box came in the mail addressed to Michael. I opened it up and inside, I found an old rusty horseshoe! There was no explanation or note with it." Was this Michael's way of telling his parents he is all right?

Gail has studied everything she could get her hands on regarding the afterlife since she was in junior high. After their son's accident, it was a natural transition for them to want to know more about the other side.

Eric and Gail, along with Dori Spence, are certified paranormal investigators based in Longmont. They are qualified to investigate a business, home, or other area to determine if there is paranormal activity.

Eric operates a variety of instruments to aid in their investigations. He is the one who wants solid evidence. He is not a psychic, but in addition to his instruments, he also relies upon his sight, hearing, and sense of smell, changes in temperature, movement, or abnormal energies.

All three strive to detect and measure electromagnetic fields in buildings where they sense strong energies. Dori has the ability to see and talk to the ghosts she finds.

When the trio enters a building, they separate and cover the entire layout then reconvene to compare notes and most often, they find that each of them separately detects something in the same areas and the fact they have not influenced each other leads them to believe they have discovered some legitimate paranormal activity.

Recycled Energy

Dori Spence explained her theory of recycled energy: "If a homeowner reports that every evening at 5 p.m., a woman comes down the staircase, recycled energy may be the reason. It was the habitual walking down the staircase at 5 p.m. every evening that created the energy." Spence said, "the mind can play tricks and make a person visualize a woman in a long, flowing gown, for example. In reality, the homeowner senses the recycled energy left there when the staircase walker was in a physical form. Our energy field never goes away, even after we have moved on."

That is why Spence often blindfolds herself or turns the lights out when she senses a spiritual presence. She does not want her imagination taking over and creating a spiritual being when all that remains is actually only the energy from that earthly life.

A secret kept by the person who has passed or unfinished business by that person will keep his spirit from leaving this world until he can communicate to a live person. Sometimes, the spirit simply wants to set the record straight or inform earthly beings about others who should not be lost and forgotten after passing to the other side.

Imperial Hotel

The Imperial Hotel was built in 1881 on the northwest corner of Third and Main. The occupants of a second floor apartment in the Imperial asked Jones and Spence to check out their place. The apartment dwellers suspected that they were living with spirits of some kind because they continually sensed someone in the bathroom and they often heard a little girl's voice in the bedroom.

When Dori first entered the apartment and walked around, she sensed something in the bedroom and upon walking into that room, briefly saw twin beds with a little girl curled up on one, crying, and a dead girl stretched out on the other bed. She said the emotional energy filling that bedroom was so dense, it felt just like it must have been when the little girl died many years ago.

At this point, Dori turned off the lights and blindfolded herself. She does this when she doesn't want anything to interfere with her intuitive abilities. It also keeps her mind from playing tricks on here by making her see things that aren't there.

Spirits have hung around the historic Imperial Hotel to tell their story.

Next, Dori saw another little girl crouched behind the bathroom door. She also saw a man come through the door where the shower was now located.

The little girl was the cleaning lady's granddaughter. She was not supposed to be in the bathroom. Her grandmother told her to stay in the living room while she worked. She didn't obey her grandmother and happened to be in a spot where she saw the man come in from what was the fire escape. He planned to rob the apartment until the unsuspecting child said hello to the man. Then he became frightened and fled.

When they investigated, the trio found evidence of a door concealed behind the shower. The door opening was closed off and covered with sheet rock. When they checked behind the building in the alley, they found where the fire escape attached to the outside wall. The concealed door connected to the fire escape from inside the apartment.

No one knew about this event but, fortunately, Dori saw and heard the little girl speak. The ghostly little girl remained in the room until she could tell someone who would understand what happened.

A downtown gourmet kitchen store

The alley also yielded other secrets to the investigators. Dori walked the alley to the entrance behind a gourmet kitchen shop. It is no longer in business, but at the time it was, the store's owner told Dori about things mysteriously moving around the shop and there was no explanation for it.

For example, there was a mug tree placed inside the back door displaying a large assortment of cookie cutters. When a grouchy customer, whom no one ever wanted to wait on, came in the back door, a rooster cookie cutter literally jumped off the shelf and hit her. Would the police file read, "victim assaulted by a deadly cookie cutter?"

There was another incident involving a set of shelves on the other side of the back door opposite the cookie cutters. Among the items displayed, there was a margarita pitcher and six glasses on a tray. When the owner walked through the back door one morning, she found the margarita pitcher and two glasses sitting on the floor. They had not simply fallen to the floor because they were sitting upright as though someone had carefully placed them there. However, no one had been in the store overnight until the owner opened the back door that morning.

Dori continued her investigation of the kitchen store by returning one night. She did not sense the mischievous spirit in the shop but, when she went down into the basement, she detected a funny little window boarded over. She determined it was the former coal shoot. She went out into the alley and sat down quietly to see if she could find anyone. Shortly, she saw a shadowy man looking like he might have been a vagrant. He said he was a hobo and used to enter the hotel through the coal shoot in the old days. He said he quit going into the hotel when it "got too deadly in there." Dori did not know what he meant by that.

Dickens Opera House

The spirit also told her, he and other homeless transients went over to the Dickens Opera House at 302 Main Street where they could stay the night, if they left the next morning before anyone came.

An older woman ghost sat in a rocking chair in front of the dressing rooms of the Dickens Opera House reading stories to children. During the busy days of the opera house, Grandmotherly volunteers read to the child actors to help them stay calm; the women also herded the kids onto stage on the proper cue.

The hobo told her that others like him, all men, except for Peter O'Toole's crazy sister, stayed in the theater. Peter O'Toole, who worked in the theater, had little money to provide for his sister, so he dressed her in costumes he found there. We bet she had the most interesting wardrobe in town.

Dickens invited homeless to seek shelter at night at the Opera House in exchange for their cleaning up the place.

Dori visited the Dickens Opera House for a performance and while waiting for the music to start, spirit of a short Irish guy appeared to her from the stage singing *Danny Boy*.

The hobo also told Dori that Dickens welcomed him and his friends to spend nights in the opera house, if they agreed to clean up the place. Dickens allowed them to take any items left behind, even jewelry forgotten by the inebriated customers. Finders, keepers! The hobos, who were mostly Irish, eagerly waited to ham it up on stage the moment the theater emptied.

The vagabond hobos were also guests in the Great Western Hotel located in between Third and Kimbark, built in 1919, to house the sugar mill workers. F.M. Downer and N.C. Sullivan built the sugar mill and the Great Western Hotel. Note they used identical bricks in each structure.

Portrait of W.H. Dickens hangs in the Dickens Opera House Building.

Java Coffee Shop

A server at the Java Coffee Shop, which is located on the ground level of the Imperial Hotel, has reported seeing a man in his fifties, dressed in work clothes, when she opened the shop and was totally alone. She saw him on three different occasions. Each time, the man was sorting through a pile of newspapers kept on a table for customers. As soon as the server spotted him, he disappeared.

A ghostly customer likes to read the newspapers furnished at the Java Stop Coffee Shop.

St. Stephens Church

Built in 1881 at 470 Main Street, was the first Episcopal Church in Longmont. The church used to have a rectory and a second story attached to it. The investigative trio checked out the building for any paranormal activity.

Some time before Gail, Eric, and Dori visited St. Stephen's, an artist named Barbara Stone had set up her studio in the back of the church.

When the threesome arrived at St. Stephens, they detected a lot of spiritual energy, first, at the altar and next, in the east corner of the church. Dori asked Eric to step over to the altar because she wanted him to check out something. They usually don't confer with each other until an investigation is finished, but this time was different. She asked him if he sensed anything

St. Stephens Church – home of the wandering minister and mysterious hints of incense scenting the air.

around the altar and he said he smelled a strong presence of incense and suddenly, it faded away.

Dori also saw a ghostly clothesline extended across the windows on the east side. On it, there was a shadowy deacon's coat hanging upside down and next to it was one child's pinafore. They were hung there to dry in front of the open window. Barbara Stone told Dori that one day, when she took her camera out of the bag, it went off accidentally, taking a picture through the pocket of the bag. The film captured the image of a child's pinafore. Thus confirming what Dori observed. Sometimes a camera will pick up something that is invisible to the human eye.

While outside, Dori spotted the ghostly former priest walking around the church property.

The Callahan House

Local Channel 3 taped the team investigating the Callahan House. located on the northeast corner of Third and Terry. The camera must have bothered the spirits, because they made it difficult to complete the taping. The camera operator brought four battery packs with him to power his camcorder. Each one usually lasted 45 minutes. "Someone" drained the power from all four of the battery packs within a very short time. The Gail, Eric, and Dori team found three ghosts that night. Perhaps the Callahan spirits are a bit camera shy...

The Callahan house is home to spirits who tried to sabotage a television event to protect their privacy.

The Elite Barber Shop

Built in 1906 at 339 Main Street, the Elite Barbershop could be Shorty's Barbershop. Even though he is no longer of this world, Shorty still hangs around to keep an eye on things. One night, Dori was leading twelve people on one of her ghost tours around the downtown area. They stopped at the barber shop and peered in. After a few moments, Spence headed on across the street but discovered she had lost all but five of her group. The remaining members stayed behind to continue peering into the barbershop.

Suddenly, they were yelling, "We saw him, we saw him!" Each of them described seeing the ghostly figure in a "butcher's apron" standing between the two barber chairs. The shadowy being was six feet, two inches tall, middle aged and balding. One of the seven said, "He had nice eyes." That's comforting!

Dori said the group consisted of very reliable people including a couple of school board members, a doctor and wife, a minister,

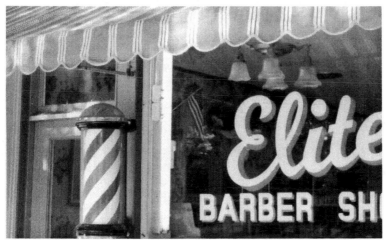

Many regular customers greet the barbers with "Is Shorty Here Today?" Shorty remains popular even though he appears from the other side these days.

etc. When five or more people report seeing the same phenomenon, she considers the sighting valid.

Dori came up with her own proof. When she was standing at the barbershop window looking in, she took three photos in succession. Each photo revealed a white filmy figure moving consistently further to the right side of the shop.

The next day, Dori returned to the barbershop to tell the owner what she and her group discovered. She began telling her story slowly, afraid of the reaction she might receive, and then the barber said, "Oh, that's Shorty. We have his picture hanging on the wall."

Since then, when she leads tours by the barbershop, they always stop to look at the picture on the wall. Longtime customers greet the barbers by asking, "Is Shorty here today?" Shorty is a very important part of the Elite Barber Shop even though he does not cut hair anymore. He left the shop in 1999 and died two years later. The apron the ghostly barber was observed wearing was a traditional barber's apron, not a butcher's.

When you visit, the tidy little shop will take you back in time with its old style chairs and friendly atmosphere. No wonder Shorty is staying on. If you don't see him, pay your respects to his photograph on the wall.

Vance Brand Civic Auditorium

Edison is the name of the auditorium spirit because he does many strange things to the electrical system. There are no explanations for the electrical snafus except there may be some gentle sabotage from beyond.

Word is the ghost is a janitor who died when the balcony collapsed on him during construction.

Students have reported cold spots, lights turning on and off and strange noises occurring. One student was feeling uneasy and spotted a strange figure in the back of the balcony watching him. Another witness reported a ghostly dog that scared him and his friend so much the boys escaped into a storage room. They felt the dog was following them and then he suddenly disappeared. Many times, people hear footsteps on the catwalk during performances; yet, no one has ever seen the human form to go with them.

In addition, auditorium chairs move as though some unseen occupant is getting up or sitting down.

Who's Behind the Eightball?

A few years ago, a young man named Yancy died suddenly of heart failure. After his funeral, his buddies decided they would play a pool game and drink a shot in honor of Yancy. They met at a local pool hall where they had played many times before.

The men racked up the balls and when they broke the first time, the eight ball rolled directly into the pocket. The guys racked the balls up again. The second time, the eight ball rolled into the pocket. They all said that this couldn't happen again. The third time...you guessed it, the eight ball rolled into the pocket. All of his friends thought Yancy was sending them a farewell so they drank a toast to him and went home.

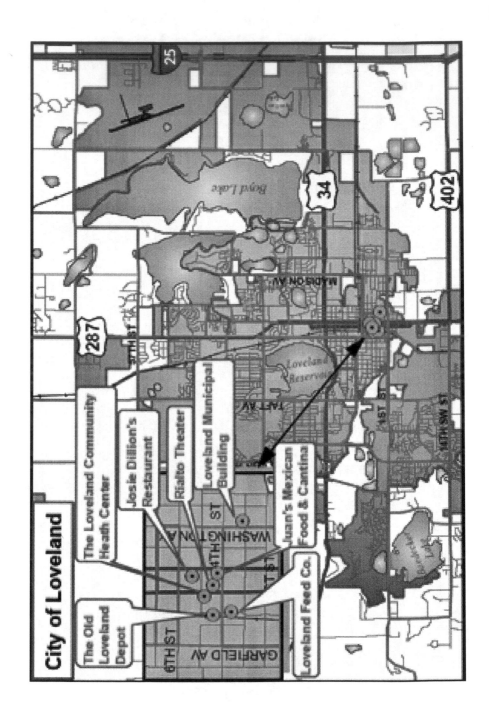

Loveland

Loveland is a front range community where the arts,
agriculture, and business coexist.
The collection of historical characters and their spirits claim
their place too.

Barbara Scott and her partner, Dori Spence conduct ghost tours in downtown Loveland. Barbara is an energy therapist and Dori is the paranormal investigator introduced in the Longmont chapter of this book. Both Dori and Barbara can see the spirits or ghosts of dead people.

Barbara explained how she and Dori unearthed the ghost stories they cover on their tours. "When we first visit a town, we walk the town and talk to people to see if they have any stories. We are also aware and can pick up stories. Dori is a psychic who has the ability to channel and I work with energies.

We walked down the alley behind the Rialto Theater a couple of times and finally got a story from a man we sensed in the alley. Alleys were actually streets in earlier days. We asked the man why he was there and he said he was there because he wanted us to realize that some people lived in the alleys in earlier days. They were the cooks, cleaners and other laborers.

Sometimes they give their story, and it comes in first person and sometimes it comes in as a story from somebody else telling us. Therefore, it just depends. When we're processing what we are receiving in our heads, we actually hear if there is a difference in vocabulary or manner of speech. Anyway, when we finally got the man's story, he said he wanted us to be aware of the people living behind the buildings in the alleys as well as those who enter through the front doors.

He also told about the people who used to live in the apartment building in that alley. He said that in those times, there were more people who lived there than paid rent.

The alley people invented a game they called Jackamore, as a diversion from their hard lives. They drew lines across the dirt and picked stones to throw between them. The players got so many points, depending upon where the stones landed. The most points were earned for the greatest distance."

Barbara said, "Most of the time when spirits tell us something, they are trying to correct a misperception of their history. They also may want to add some important detail to their story.

The stories come through in the spirits' language. The alley people tried to entice the people who were coming out of the Rialto during intermission for a "smoke" to play Jackamore. The term "smoke" is not used today, but we hear them speaking in the voice of their time. The theatergoers responded to the alley people and joined them in Jackamore. They didn't know what they were getting into, however.

The alley people had stones they practiced with and knew they could fly far. The people who came out from the Rialto would go in the alley and try to find the prettiest, smoothest rocks they could. The pretty, smooth rocks usually didn't fly as well as the duller, flat ones. The alley people easily won the games against the theatergoers.

We asked, what is Jackamore? It took three trips into the alley before we got that story. He said that the name of the man who made up the game was Jack. The game was named Jackamore because there was always somebody who wanted to play more."

The Rialto Theater

The Rialto Theater supporters celebrated the grand opening in May 1920. The construction cost was $100,000, which was a staggering sum for that day. Loveland businessman William Vorreiter wanted a theater to rival the modern showcase theaters in Denver. The Rialto did just that.

Jan Sawyer, the theater manager, has heard the legends regarding the worker falling off the scaffolding during construction to his death and the other about the vaudeville actress dying in her dressing room. Sawyer doesn't know whether these stories are true or not.

She does know, there are spirits in the theater, and is very grateful they are there. She and the staff feel protected by them and appreciate the positive spiritual energy in the theater.

Little, unexplained things happen frequently that convince her that their ghostly companions are living happily at the Rialto. She has felt a presence pass her on the steps, just as she would if a person brushed shoulders as they passed when going in opposite directions up or down. No one was there.

Sawyer has felt a hand pressure on her shoulders as though someone was scooting behind her and touched her on the way. No one was there. The staff has heard voices in the theater and...no one was there.

Missing objects are a common occurrence. She doesn't know whether she and the staff lose items by themselves or have other help to do so. Keys sitting on a desk will disappear for a long period, and then reappear where they were originally. Sawyer said, "The ghosts are convenient to blame, but we don't know if they do it or not."

Workers hardwired a communications system into the building and set it up for communication between backstage, projection room, box office, and elsewhere. "We plug headphones into the wall outlet to send and receive." One night, she and an employee heard someone send a message on the intercom, "Fairy tales do come true." The voice said nothing else. Of course, a search for the person talking over the system turned up no one. No one was there. Sawyer even asked a technician if a cell phone or walkie talkie could have broken into their system. He said he didn't think so, because the system was hard wired into the building, not wireless. Sawyer is respectful to the elusive spirit and simply thanked him for the message.

A couple of years ago, Sawyer and her daughter, along with a news reporter and two paranormal investigators from Denver, spent an evening together hunting spirits.

When the group was checking out the Rialto, she took them to the projection room, which is always locked. Sawyer unlocks it several times daily with the same key that she was using that night. After several attempts, the lock did not open. Sawyer knew she had the correct key and that the lock was not broken so, she simply asked spirits for their permission to enter the booth. The lock clicked open immediately.

Once inside the projection booth, the paranormal investigators reported they detected a great deal of electromagnetic energy

Spirits are very active in the projection room at the Rialto Theater.

and that there were a number of energy spots, presumably coming from spiritual energy. Later, a photograph of the room revealed several orbs indicating energy from something.

The Rialto has made it through many financial and cultural changes since that grand opening in 1920. The struggles are over now and the popular theater is doing very well financially because it fulfills a definite niche in the community. Sawyer said that she feels the spirits are benign and peaceful now because the theater is a peaceful, happy place. When the theater was in survival mode and things were chaotic, the spirits were also unsettled.

Visit the Rialto and you will feel the happiness and peace for yourself and thank the spirits, as Sawyer does, for their presence and the positive energy they bring to it.

Orbs

Orbs are picked up very easily by digital cameras, causing many to believe they have caught one on film when, in fact, the images are of accumulated dust or reflections. Many spots found in photos are mistaken for orbs.

According to Gail and Eric, a true orb is a concentration of electromagnetic energy, presumably from a spirit. An authentic orb appears on film as a solid white object

The Jones's use both digital and 35 mm SLR cameras, so they have the use of a negative for evidence. If they believe they have photographed an orb, they take the negative to a lab to verify that the film is unaltered and to determine that the object photographed is genuine.

A digital camera is more sensitive but there is no negative to analyze for authenticity.

Photo of an orb.

The Loveland Feed Co. 343 Railroad North

Barbara and Dori made an amazing discovery when walking by the old grain elevator on Third and Railroad Avenue.

Fire destroyed the mill in 1882. The new mill opened in 1891. The elevator was a stop for the railroad to load grain onto the trains.

Barbara said, "Dori and I were walking to the elevator and I said, you know there's a whole group of guys standing up along the side of the building. I have the ability to see the spirits and there were a lot of them. Hobos were everywhere during the depression. They arrived at the elevator every day to see if any farmers needed help. We realized that's what they did during the depression, the hobos were there to work. They stood by the building to wait for work or catch the train.

The east side of the old Loveland Feed and Grain Co. Hobo spirits from days gone by still wait in the shadows as they did during the depression era.

The day we were doing the walk around that place and the hobos were standing there, we were able to see a ghostly someone feeding thirty or forty stray cats.

We continued walking around the building on the west side where there are some windows. I said to Dori, 'I really think there is someone in there.'"

She said, "Oh yeah."

"He was just backing away from the window and trying not to be seen. Dori went to ask the ghost if he had a story he might want to share."

He said, "Get out," or something like that. Next, he said, "And this means you."

"We saw a sign that said the same thing. It was almost as if he was trying to protect the place," Barbara said.

Barbara does not know what would happen to the hobo spirits if the grain elevator is torn down and replaced by condominiums. Would that be a good time for someone to aid those people and felines with ascension into the afterlife?

Barbara said, "We saw those people standing there again on one of our tours and as we were talking about the hobos, one of the women on the tour gave us more information. She told us that when she was a young girl, she went to the park and recreation area south of the elevator. She said that during the depression, a hobo camp was located there. The woman also said she used to go down there and visit with those guys in their camp near the river."

Eddie

Helen Colella's beloved husband Eddie died after a long illness.

On the night he died in a local nursing home, his daughter stayed at the family home to man the phone and keep the out-of-state family abreast of the situation.

The girl knew her father died before Helen called her because Eddie appeared on the back porch, leaning over the railing in his favorite spot. Did he return home to say goodbye to his daughter and see his home for one last time?

Helen often felt and saw his presence in the house as shadows flashed by her. She felt him standing behind her when she was cooking. She also saw his wavy, water-like figure in different areas of the house.

The family dog sensed Eddie's presence too. He often stared for long periods at the computer or other places where Eddie spent time.

Since Helen moved to a new home, she knows he is near but his presence isn't nearly as intense as before. Hopefully, Eddie is at peace now that Helen has found her way to a new life.

Josie Dillon's Restaurant (closed)

Josie Dillon is an historical figure from Colorado mining days. Linda Caplan and Kathy Thelan researched Josie Dillon before opening their country themed restaurant and decided her name was a fitting one for their establishment which was located in the 500 block of North Cleveland. Josie Dillon's was actually ahead of its time with menu selections. They introduced the first bagels to Loveland customers who wondered what those "boggles" were. Linda and Kathy operated Josie Dillon's from 1981-1989.

The two women had a third partner—his name was Barlow. They didn't see him much, if at all. They saw his tidy handiwork often, however...

Linda and Kathy decorated their place with nicely framed historic pictures covered in glass, plus other accessories that established the atmosphere they wanted to create.

Linda said that they started their workdays at 3 a.m. in order to bake and prepare food. There was no one else in the building at that hour, but Linda and Kathy often heard noises from the basement. Both women were early Stephen King fans so it was natural for them to name the elusive presence Barlow after their favorite character in the novel *Salem's Lot*.

Kathy's brother heard the stories about the basement noises and one day, insisted the twosome join him in the basement to check out the coal bin where they were sure, the spirit lived. They hardly ever went into the old musty basement but this day, they did. The wooden door to the coal bin was partly stuck because the concrete had settled over the years. When they opened it, the door creaked and at that point, the two women bolted out of the basement leaving Kathy's brother to take care of himself and Barlow.

After that, Barlow started taking the pictures off the walls. Did they set him free to do his mischief when they opened the coal bin door?

Barlow was not present everyday. Sometimes he left them alone for several months. He came around in the wintertime to let everyone know he was back by moving things. They set the tables to prepare for the following day and always placed fresh flowers on each table. When they entered the restaurant to start the day, things often greeted Linda and Kathy on the tabletops moved all over. That's not all they found...

They hosted special parties, such as their annual Halloween bash, and could always count on finding the pictures off the wall the next morning. The pictures were always lying face down on the carpet. Barlow lined the pictures up very neatly in a row. The glass was never broken. The nails in the walls were always intact. Linda said that they knew the pictures had not fallen off by themselves, because Barlow aligned them on the carpet and always placed them face down. Every time they returned the morning after a party to clean up, it was inevitable that Barlow had moved the pictures to the floor. They don't know if he liked the parties or merely wanted to remind them of his presence.

Barlow became part of the restaurant because the customers got into his stories too. The customers believed the stories about the presence named Barlow and never said Linda and Kathy were making things up. Barlow was a friendly spirit and the women were never afraid when they heard his noises coming from the basement in the early morning hours.

Linda and Kathy sold Josie Dillon's in 1989 to a friend who wanted to carry on the established theme and menu. When Linda returned to visit the restaurant, there were no more Barlow stories. Maybe he left at the same time they did.

Linda believes that if a spirit likes you, it will hang out with you. Barlow was a fun and friendly third partner in Josie Dillon's restaurant.

Juan's Mexican Food and Cantina

Juan Moresco claims there are several ghosts haunting his restaurant at 128 East Fourth Street. George, one of the spirits is credited with shattering glasses, flickering lights, unplugging the ice machine and dropping fourteen bottles of tequila from a shelf without breaking even one!

Jealous Shelley might be a prostitute from the days when the building was a brothel. She rubs against people and fills the room with the scent of her strong perfume.

Dennis, the restaurant's former cook died in a car accident and liked the restaurant so much he decided to stay on for a while.

Moresco's son Gary, who died in 2004, along with an additional unidentified spirit complete the ghostly group. Moresco said he knows when the spirits are around because his skin crawls.

When a server said she didn't believe in ghosts, a shelf of lightweight plastic cooking equipment dropped on her head. Now, she is a believer.

The Loveland Community Health Center

Formerly the home of The Daily Reporter-Herald, it is located at 450 North Cleveland.

According to an October 30, 2002 article in the Reporter Herald, a receptionist at the Center was working early in the morning and thought she was alone. As she walked through a dark hallway, she felt someone behind her. As she passed a window, she saw the reflection of a woman with long hair following her closely. She thought it was the clinic manager trying to scare her. When she turned around to confront the manager, she saw nothing.

Workers have named their spirit Mattie or Matilda. She hides charts, makes loud noises, and disconnects phones.

When the Reporter Herald was located in the building, staffers reported numerous cold spots, scary sounds, and chairs rolling across the floor.

The Loveland Municipal Building, formerly Washington School

Workers hear children's laughter echoing through the halls. Cleaning crews hear the laughter when no children are there. The sounds would be happy ones if made by living children. However, the laughter the cleaning crews hear, unnerves them. Would that be the reason for the high turnover or would it be because of the doors opening and closing for no reason. Add to that, the moving trashcans and the footsteps with no one in sight. We won't even mention the scary elevator. The stairs are handy and visitors might want to use them. The building, located at 500 East Third, was Washington School from 1905 to 1973, which is plenty of time to collect a few wayward spirits.

The municipal building, formerly the Washington Elementary School is home to hyperactive ghost children.

The Old Railroad Depot

It just seems like the Depot, located at 409 North Railroad Avenue, should be haunted, given its long history and all. Dori Spence verified it by identifying a child named Nathan who may have become sick and died from something that made him cough. Another version is that Nathan's parents abandoned him at the Depot when they became ill and unable to care for him.

Dori talked to another Depot ghost named Jack Daniels, who said that he might have run booze during Prohibition.

There is the tunnel that once ran from the Depot to the Elks Club Building at 103 East Fourth. Booze runners used the tunnel secretly to move it from the Depot to the Elks Club.

Scary Appearances

There are so few malevolent spirits, that it is particularly frightening when encountering one.

A retailer on North Cleveland reported two different apparitions have visited her. The first happened ten years ago, when the owner was alone in the store after closing. She was working and felt a presence. When she turned around, she saw a young girl, about 12 years old in a long dress and high top shoes. She was peaceful and nonthreatening to the owner.

The second experience occurred one year later, when the owner was working in her office after hours and was alone in the store. The figure was very frightening. He was dressed in black and wore a black cloak that covered him so she could not make out his silhouette. She felt he was an evil old man.

There have been no apparitions showing themselves to anyone in the store since. The history of the building as a former morgue lends itself to being the home of many ghosts. Luckily, the owner has seen only two of them...

The Darkroom Interloper

An employee at the same retail store recounted her husband's experience in an ad agency on North Cleveland. The husband had no belief in the afterlife and certainly not in ghosts. He was working in the darkroom late one night. There was a knock on the door and, not wanting to expose his work to light, he shouted, "Wait a minute." When he answered the door, there was no one there. There was no one else in the building with him that night.

The next day, he asked everyone at the agency if any of them had stopped in the night before. No one had visited him the night before. That is, no one from this side.

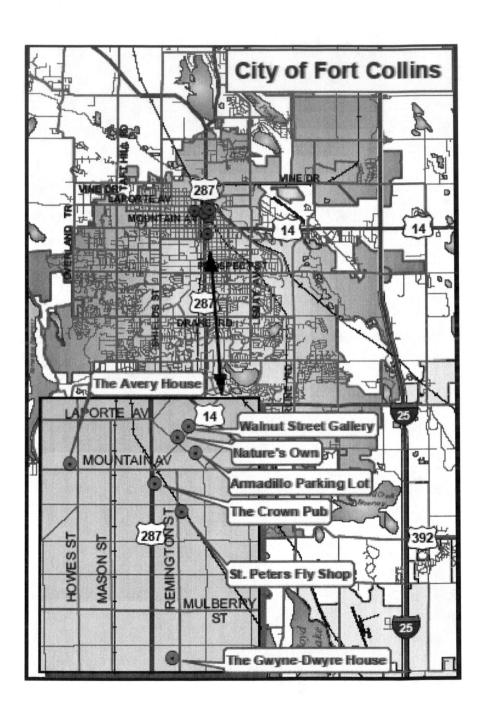

Fort Collins

Fort Collins is a community loaded with enough facilities, culture, commerce, sports activities and overall beauty to make everyone living there happy. There are numerous stories of ghost and spirits who greatly add to the town's overall appeal.

Library Park, 201 Peterson Street

The name changed from Lincoln Park in the early seventies. Voters determined the new library should be located within that city block area.

There was a huge controversy over the library placement and size. The library design on stilts is the result of a creative idea of inverting the floor plan and placing the larger area on the second floor. The space taken up by the first floor met the covenants, and all was in compliance. Apparently, so much time and energy was spent on the issues surrounding the library construction that no attention was given to less concrete details...

A group of citizens was concerned about the negative atmosphere in the library and asked Kim Pentecost to clear it and the surrounding park. She learned no one had ever asked the land if it was willing to receive the building and, as a result, things did not feel positive within the library or elsewhere in the area.

Kim was teaching a class about intuitive techniques at the same time, and thought it would make a terrific community project for the students. It was a good thing she had help from her students, because the project turned out to be larger than originally thought.

The class looked at all the buildings on the property. No one had paid any attention to the historic buildings transferred to the site before. It was important to do so now because those old structures retained a tremendous amount of energy from the lifetime of use by folks long gone.

Kim said, "There are generally a lot of ghosts in a library because there is so much history, along with emotional energy, tragedy, joy, death, and love in the books and other items stored there. Libraries attract many interesting things, some are good and some are not."

Ghosting 101

Kim Pentecost is an Intuitive Consultant who has consulted with private citizens and public officials on many subjects including the basics of ghosting 101.

First, according to Kim, when a person dies and becomes a ghost, that action is called ghosting. It happens primarily if someone has unfinished business on the planet.

Kim said," Ghosts want one of three things: they want to get a message out to our world, or they're very fearful of something so they may act very mean and scary in order to drive us away and continue to live their reality. Last, some ghosts want to get our attention, and they will do things such as slam doors, knock pictures off walls, etc., because they want our help to ascend to the afterlife."

Ghosts recognize who can see them.

"When a person has been a ghost for a long period of time, they forget or lose the ability to fully ascend to the other side. Therefore, they want our attention in order for us to help them in their ascension," she said.

When the class started working, she taught the students the necessary steps to put them in communication with the spirit of the land. They conducted a lot of healing work on the land.

When building the library, there was so much conflict that no one focused on the land. This resulted in creating a chaotic atmosphere.

The students and Kim brought blessings from Spirit and walked the perimeter of the whole block. They also went inside the library but did not disturb the staff. They simply carried on with their work. The group helped some ghosts who were stuck to ascend. In short, they conducted a spiritual cleansing of the entire land area and all the buildings on it.

She said people reported to her the library felt so much better after that. She feels it speaks well for the Fort Collins community that some citizens were concerned enough to seek her help.

Enlightened developers who are aware of the concepts of spiritual energy often ask Kim Pentecost or other intuitives to walk an area to be under construction. The intuitives clear energies that could interfere with the lives of the occupants of the proposed structures.

Centennial High School

Centennial High School, located at 330 East Laurel Street, is said to be haunted by a young girl who fell to her death on the large wooden staircase running down the center of the building. Many students have reported hearing a girl's voice and they sense someone is watching them.

Helmshire Hall, formerly Helmshire Inn, 1204 S.College

A worker claims ghosts have undone his work on the third floor after he cleaned all the rooms. Closed curtains opened again and beds were torn apart. Toilets also flushed and all of this happened to him when he was positive he was the only person present in the building.

The basement is home to its own apparitions. Do the third floor inhabitants visit the basement from time to time just to keep the humans alert and spooked?

The Ramada Inn, formerly The Holiday Inn Holidome, 3836 East Mulberry

There's an ominous ghost of a man in the top of the northwest wing. Maybe he's friendly after you meet him.

The ghost of a woman looks out from one of the rooms especially when children are playing in the swimming pool. Sort of a vaporous lifeguard.

The most active apparition is the little girl who takes key cards from the guests' rooms and blasts the air conditioning in the room across the hall from the king suite.

Children's Mercantile

The Crown Pub and the Children's Mercantile at 111
N. College are part of the History Museum's annual
Halloween Tour.

When David Heck offered to paint the bright blue accent stripe
on the wall for his wife and her partner who are owners of
Children's Mercantile, he had no idea he might be upsetting the
resident spirit.

David was working alone in the building at about 4 a.m. He
set up a tall stepladder in the rear of the store near the old freight
elevator. The restroom was right below the ladder.

First, David smelled something like the scent after a rain. Before
he knew what was happening, the paint bucket flew out of his
hand. He kept his grip on the wire handle while the pail fell.

"It just blew my mind that none of the merchandise was
damaged by the spilled blue paint. The bucket ripped from the

A spirit who is very busy, but harmless reigns at Children's Mercantile.

handle, which was still in my hand. Then there was a flash of static electricity. If I just dropped the bucket myself, there would have been a lot of damage. The paint would have splashed all over everything. It just gave me the willies," he said.

The next morning, back in the corner where David's ladder was set up, the bathroom door lock broke and the door jammed with Shelly Dragon, one of the owners trapped inside. They had to break down the door to free her.

There have been other incidents in the rear of the store particularly, with the bathroom. Maybe the spirit doesn't like blue...

St. Peter's Fly Shop

Employees at St. Peter's Fly Shop at 202 Remington have reported cold breezes in closed rooms and unexplained voices. Employees also report setting items in one place at night and finding them moved to a new position the next morning.

The building that the fly shop occupies was once "The House of Mayors", as it was home to many of Fort Collins' early mayors. The carriage house in back, which is now apartments, was the McHugh Hospital. The hospital had a rear door that served as a delivery door where hearses moved the dearly departed in and out.

Museum of Contemporary Art, 201 S. College

It was the original post office building on the former site of the Camp Collins Graveyard, built in 1912.

During the time of Camp Collins, many soldiers died of disease or injury rather than from battle wounds. It is surprising that a building set on a former graveyard does not experience unusual events. Builders moved the bodies of the men to a cemetery before beginning construction. Officials moved the vagabond bodies again to make way for a housing development. There are no reports of ghostly soldiers hanging on through their two moves.

The Crown Pub

The Crown Pub,. 134 S. College, and the former Brotherton's Office Supply shared the same building. Reports from the History Museum files reveal that only the Crown Pub side is haunted. An employee at the pub reported a wine bottle flying from a wine rack, hitting the bar and smashing on the floor.

Two other employees were sitting at the bar after closing one night and the kitchen door swung open by itself. They could see a filmy figure walking through the kitchen. Both men got up and went to the kitchen, one walked through each of the two doors. There was no one there. There are numerous reports of doors slamming and things flying off the kitchen walls. The apartments on the second floor have a very high turnover rate for unknown reasons...

Avery House, 328 West Mountain

It has become the most publicly recognized home in Fort Collins. The history of the Avery House certainly qualifies it for some sort of spiritual activity, given the history of the people who lived there. Frank Avery, one of the city's founding fathers, built the house in 1879 for $3000, right after he and his wife were married. He also built the bank building in 1897, which is Beaujo's Pizza today.

Frank Avery's daughter married Newton Crose, a young lawyer whose office was in the Avery Block. William Ryan was a client who found himself heavily in debt with no means to pay. He was unhappy with his attorney Crose's advice and threatened Crose several times. On the morning of August 14, 1914, the two were to meet in Crose's office. It must have been an unpleasant meeting because Ryan left abruptly, returning half an hour later with a gun and shooting Crose in his little finger. When Crose tried to run away, Ryan shot him in the leg and then twice in the stomach. That did it. Crose finally died from the multiple wounds and police arrested Ryan.

The official position of the Avery organization is there has been no paranormal activity in the house. There are many individuals who have experienced events there and know what they have seen...

Ryan's confession was, "I guess I know I've killed him. He ruined me and I've ruined him."

That was not the end of the Avery dramas.

Frank's brother, William died on June 2, 1890 of a suspicious illness. His doctor wanted to perform an autopsy, but William's widow would have none of it. Things became a little more suspicious nine days later, when the grieving widow married William's law partner, Frank Millington, in Denver.

Millington's neighbors reported seeing Mrs. Avery, wearing a heavy black veil, sneaking up his back stairs before the murder. Because of that information, the family had William's body exhumed. The autopsy revealed traces of arsenic.

The law caught up with the former Mrs. Avery and her new husband. Authorities brought them back to Fort Collins on the train. Most of the town turned out to greet the nabbed couple when they returned to the city of their imperfect murder.

Did the townspeople want to check out the murder suspects firsthand? There are no secrets in a small town....

In the early 1980's, the Avery House was home to city offices and The Fort Collins Magazine owned by Eleanor Gale. Employees often reported strange happenings. Once, a light fixture crashed to the floor. However, when repairmen came to fix it, they found that the screws holding it in place were still intact.

One evening, the magazine editor and other staff members were meeting in the front room upstairs and sharing eerie stories of a male ghost some of them saw walking around the house at night. It was difficult to get any of the magazine staff to work late after they heard that story.

Tenants reported leaving for the night and returning the next morning to find the things on their desks rearranged. No one had been in the house overnight.

A local realtor said that she worked in the Avery House when city offices were located there. She was alone in the house one night and saw a cat in the doorway of the sewing room upstairs from the corner of her eye. The orange and white cat appeared very real before he vanished. There was no live cat in the house at the time.

One night, a tenant was leaving and attempting to lock the downstairs door. Something or someone did not want the door to close. The tenant could feel someone tugging on the door, but he could see no one there. Eventually, the pulling on the door stopped, it slammed shut, and the door handle fell off.

The governing board of the Avery House is adamant that there are no verified ghost sightings in the house. There are numerous reports from individuals that contradict that statement.

The strongest energies have reportedly come from the kitchen pantry and the middle bedroom upstairs. The bedroom is reputed to have belonged to a young girl whom observers feel is very unhappy. The front sitting parlor is also a site where several have sensed a presence.

The Golding-Dwyre House, 649 Remington

Bonnie Shetler, a psychologist in private practice, is the long-time owner of the Golding Dwyer House now converted to offices. She recounted her intriguing story: "Back in the early to mid eighties, one of the women who worked at night in the house would say to me, you know this place is haunted, don't you?" "But I kind of blew it off, at first." Bonnie said.

"One night, the same tenant was working down on the main floor and the radio that she kept in her office upstairs in the front bedroom just went on by itself. I said clock radios do that."

She said, "It wasn't a clock radio. It just turned on."

Bonnie continued, "And then, another night the same tenant was upstairs working in her office, and the faucet in the bathroom at the end of the hall just turned on. Since she was the only one in the house, she went to the bathroom and shut it off.

Later on, another tenant, who was a massage therapist, asked if a friend coming up from Denver on business could sleep in her office. The friend did not have a place to stay. Nobody used the building on weekends, nobody else seemed to care, and I didn't care, so I said sure.

A few weeks later, the massage therapist reluctantly came into my office and said there was something she had to tell me."

The therapist said, "When finished, she came out of the bathroom, which is at the end of the hallway. It runs straight through the building and out to a balcony.

There is a door, with a window, opening to the balcony. My friend saw a silhouetted woman standing in front of the door. There was no light on in the building but the streetlight was shining behind the woman. All she saw was a woman with long hair and a dress, just standing there. It so freaked her out that she went back into the office where she was staying and slammed the door. Needless to say, she did not go to sleep the rest of the night."

Bonnie said, "Those are only the two concrete sources of ghost activity I know of."

At one point, there was some tension in the building between some of the tenants, and I was very concerned. I was working in the house one Saturday when no one else was there, and I found myself apologizing to the house saying that I was sorry this happened. I wasn't sure what the outcome would be, but it sure seemed to have an effect on the house itself. As I was apologizing, I was getting a very strong feeling that the house was sort of saying to me, don't worry about it, everything will be okay.

As I was sitting there in the front room, I saw a note pinned to my office door. I felt the house saying, 'don't worry it will be taken care of.' I looked at the note, and sure enough, it was from the individual who was the most upset. Her note said, 'I found another place'. That was what needed to happen. That fact was very clear to me, but I didn't want to tell her that.

The spirit of the Golding-Dwyre House left a precious gift behind.

I do not believe our ghost is still here. After I heard the story about the woman on the balcony, I was at a woman's retreat and met someone who was much more into the alternative experiences than I was."

She said, "Well, if you do have a ghost, chances are, she's stuck, and she needs your encouragement to go."

Bonnie said, "Soon after the retreat, I did that. She seemed like a very gentle ghost and I gave her permission to move on.

I have felt since the mid-nineties that she has not been in the house. However, she left behind some wonderful energy. I know that, just from the way people respond when they walk into the building. It is a very positive energy. This is a very ordinary house in many ways, except it does have this energy to it that is very gentle."

The ghost is the daughter of the original owner, Abner Loomis, who built the house for her when she married Charles Golding Dwyre. Effie and her husband Charles lived in the house for many years and raised their family there.

Bonnie continued, "When the Golding Dwyre grandkids came into town on a tour of researching their roots, they asked to come into the house because they spent a lot of time in it while visiting their grandparents. They wanted to see how it had changed.

I met them at the house, because I wanted to talk to them. I asked them if anyone died in the house."

They said, "Yes, their grandmother, Effie, died in the house. She caught pneumonia and was very ill for a time and they moved her downstairs." "That is now my office and she died there," Bonnie said.

"I appreciate the gift she gave us, because it really does make for a very peaceful environment for everyone. All of us do some form of therapy or work with people who are anxious about something."

Another Spirited House Story

Olivia purchased a home in Fort Collins during the eighties and almost immediately upon moving in, she began to suspect that she was sharing the house with a spirit of some kind. Things happened, there were disappearing objects, and lights turning on and off, so Olivia went to the library to research a rumor neighbors had told her, about a suicide occurring in the house. She found news items confirming the rumors about a woman ending her life while living there. Olivia returned to her house and sat down to talk to the spirit, assuring her that it was all right for her to move on, and that the house would be well taken care of. Since that time, the homeowner never experienced any more spiritual antics.

Cleaning House

A house on the edge of Old Town carried energy from early days when it was used for slave holding.

It is believed that slaves were transported through Fort Collins on their way elsewhere. While in town, the slaves were crammed into the basement of the house. There was a small heater left on in the cold basement to give them a source of warmth. Evidently, a fire started from the heater and many individuals died in that basement.

The homeowners asked Kim Pentecost and an associate to clean out the sad energy. They discovered there were some ghosts stuck, along with the grief, sadness, and death. They also noted someone had removed the stairway to the attic. Kim feels there was negative energy in the attic also. They blessed the house to help the remaining ghosts and cleared as much negative energy as they could.

Walnut Street Gallery, 217 Linden Street

The building is 105+ years old. Gallery owner Laura and Bill Everleigh's gallery haunting experiences are so varied; there is something to intrigue everyone.

Laura said when they moved into the building, they discovered an old tunnel running from their building to the holding cell under the jail.

People told the Everleighs that bad people held Indians in the basement and killed them there.

"We've had many strange happenings in the gallery," Laura said. "For example, my office is on the mezzanine level of the first floor, and one night when I was working late; I heard very loud footsteps running upstairs. I thought it was my kids coming to the gallery to talk to me. The heavy steps came running into my office. My back is to the door when I sit at my desk in the office. I turned, thinking it was Bill and the kids coming over. No one was there. That one scared me a little bit.

Many spirits ranging from a young boy to musicians long gone like to visit the Walnut Street Gallery.

We used to keep our frame samples in the back part of the gallery fastened onto sliding doors with Velcro. Those frames have literally flown off the door. Even my staff has witnessed them flying horizontally off the door. If the frame samples simply came loose, they would fall to the floor. Instead, they literally flew across the room.

The two big double doors that lead to the back room bang shut by themselves, making a loud noise.

Once, I had a very vivid dream about the gallery and those double doors. The dream began with my working late at night once again. I heard the double doors bang, so I went to open the doors to check on them. I saw all these men walking around very fast in the back room. I just closed the door quietly and left. I thought that was a very strange dream.

Laura recalled, "Shortly after that, a Coloradoan reporter, writing a feature on ghosts, brought a paranormal investigator into the gallery. When she came, I did not tell her anything. She entered the back room using one of those little pendulums, and I thought yeah, right. She went into the back room and said there was lots of energy back there and I thought, that's interesting, remembering my dream.

Next, the investigator went through our back door and into the alley.

She said, 'There is LOTS of energy back here.' The little pendulum went very horizontal and she screamed, I screamed, and we all jumped. I said, "Omigod what is it?"

She said, "There's a vortex back here!" *Ed note: A vortex is a whirling mass of energy.*

"We were outside in the alley and she said that the energy from a number of musicians was out there along with the smoke from their cigarettes. The woman did not know we work with musicians. She told me they like to hang out there because that is where my husband, Bill, smokes his cigars.

Next, the investigator came inside to the back room and then she said, "A lot of men walked back and forth in this area." I replied to her, "that's just like my dream!

I told her, I always had the feeling the footsteps I heard were from a little boy. The investigator pointed to an area and said a little boy died here in an elevator shaft. Where she pointed to, is exactly where an old elevator shaft used to be.

The investigator actually knelt down on the floor and talked to the little spirit and we haven't had any experiences with the little boy since then."

Then she pointed to the back corner of the room and she started laughing, and I asked her what was so funny.

She said, "John Entwistle (a deceased musician) is back there. And he is making this motion."

A concentration of spiritual energy swirls around the old jail house located behind the Walnut Street Gallery.

"She showed us how your arms would raise if you were wearing a cape and brought your arms up to flip it over your shoulder. She also brought one leg up to further demonstrate how he was standing, and I said I can't believe you did that!"

The investigator's statement was very surprising to Laura, who was friend of the late musician John Entwistle because she knew the last drawing that John did, was of himself in that same position.

Laura said, "I have not even seen that drawing yet but, my husband has, and he told me about it. I thought that was bizarre. We have things like that happening all the time."

Laura said, "One of my employees was setting the alarm one night while preparing to close. When she turned and looked toward the front door, she saw a cloaked figure in the doorway and it appeared to float towards her. She was horrified."

When you visit the gallery, if you're lucky, you will see much more then art...

The Armadillo Restaurant parking lot, 354 Walnut Street

Research indicates the parking lot of the restaurant is the site of one of the most historic murders in Fort Collins.

There was a house located where the parking lot of the restaurant is now. In 1888, a mill worker named James Howe came home drunk and upon meeting his wife in the doorway of their home, stabbed her to death. She stumbled out into the front yard, onto the sidewalk and died there.

The Sheriff arrested Howe shortly after. Late that night, after all lights were out, an enraged group of vigilantes broke into the jail and lynched him where the county courthouse was under construction. Thankfully, this is the only recorded lynching in Larimer County history.

Health Food Store (closed), College and Elizabeth

A ghost who looked like a mountain man loved the health food store because he loved the scents of the herbs. He just sat somewhere in the store. When customers passed by him, they shuddered from the cold chill he emitted. The storeowner knew he was in the shop the moment she saw a customer shudder from the cold.

The owner requested Kim Pentecost help the ghost to ascend. Kim went to the store, saw the spirit, and asked him if he wanted help to ascend. He said that he did not. He thought he had a purpose there, because he was protecting the store and the owner.

How to Help With Ascension

There are two ways to help a spirit who is stuck and wants to consider ascending to the afterlife:

First, Kim Pentecost said, if you have good intentions, you can set up an ascending light. Anyone can do it. It draws spirits or ghosts who have lost their way and don't know how to connect and ascend."

She cautions, "Set it up outside your house or you will have ghosts walking through your home. Call on Spirit and ask for a beam of light.

Whatever your intuition says, is the right length of time for it to be, do it. That is it. Psychic stuff is simple. People make a big deal of it. It's simple."

Several people in this book have demonstrated the second. That is, to simply talk to the spirit. Assure them it is all right to leave. Some have told the spirit they will leave it alone if the spirit behaves, and then everyone can live happily ever after. Others simply thank the spirit for being protective of the property or the people who live there. Still others ask permission to enter a particular area, promise to be respectful and thank the spirit upon leaving the area.

He was a big man dressed in leather and looked like a hunter or trapper. He focused on providing protection to the store and the owner. It was clear he didn't realize, to some extent, that he was dead. He acknowledged, after some encouragement, that people did not respond to him when he spoke to them. Some people smiled at him because they had a sense he was there. Kim went ahead and brought in a beam of light for him to ascend. He thanked her, but wanted to make sure the storeowner and her sons were going to be okay.

Kim said, "He was a very gentle and loving man. That was the first ghost I met and that was in 1990."

Spirits Like Newer Buildings Too

Contrary to what most believe, a building does not have to be old to be home to a ghost or spirit...

For example, one day, the manager of a retail store at Harmony and College was opening for the day. When she entered the store, she was met by a little girl standing inside as though she was waiting for someone. The manager said, "Hi, how did you get in here?" She walked around the counter to talk to the silent little girl, who walked away circling a display. Suddenly, there was no one there. *The shops at the Harmony College Center are not very old. Did those businesses intrude upon someone's historic resting place?*

Unfinished Business

Si Barella, a local realtor told about his father in law who died a few years ago in his home in east Fort Collins. Si's mother in law moved into an apartment and Si sold the house to a young woman. Some time later, the woman called Si to help her find a larger home. While they were checking out houses, she asked Si if anyone had died in her house. He told her about his father-in-law. She said she thought so, because one night, a small, kindly man appeared in her bedroom and was stepping in front of a row of candles. On the wall behind the candles were statues of several saints. Quickly, he was gone.

Si told her his father-in-law died in the house and that the couple were very strong Catholics and kept a personal altar in their home. There were statues of saints on the wall and candles in front of them. He also confirmed his father in law was a small, gentle man.

The woman said she was not afraid, because she could feel he was a good man and meant her no harm. The family thought he returned to finish something he needed to do.

Possible Sites For Ghost hunters

There was a tunnel running from the jail to the Silver Grille, which routed prisoners to meals without going onto the street.

There is an underground stream running through the downtown area, which Kim Pentecost believes it is a very active spiritual area. Kim has seen the doorway leading to the underground tunnel from the Walrus Ice Cream Shop. Do the spirits ever dip into the ice cream?

Livermore

Livermore was a stage stop located exactly one day's stagecoach ride from both Fort Collins and Laramie. The area is rich in history, from prehistoric dates to present day western events.

The spiritual side of that history has coexisted with the mortal side for all time and is very interesing...

The Roberts Ranch

A 20,000 acre working cattle ranch in Livermore and a focal point of local history since the first cattle were brought to it in 1873 from Texas.

Derek Roberts is the current owner of his family ranch, having inherited it from his Uncle Ernie. Derek has experienced several unexplained events in the old ranch house.

Derek's great grandparents built the family ranch using hand-hewn logs that came from the property. The Roberts used only hand tools to complete the huge task. They also built the landmark Forks Restaurant.

At one point, fire damaged the front part of the ranch house. After the fire, the front door was removed from the ranch house and installed at the Forks. The door included an etched glass window. When the house restoration was underway, the family traded doors with the Forks and the etched glass door returned to its home.

Shortly after the old door was installed in its original place on the ranch house, a brief heavy wind came up and slammed the door hard enough to break the etched glass. They have never had a wind like that before and haven't seen one since. When winds blow around the ranch, they have never blown in such a way as to catch the front door. Derek believes that something besides Mother Nature was the real cause of the door's breaking. The Roberts Ranch spirits have definite opinions about things.

When Derek and Penny Roberts were married in the summer of 1972, they were living at the ranch. They were in bed one night and Derek awoke to see someone come and stand at the foot of the bed watching them. There were no other people in the house. The silent stalker vanished while Derek was looking at him.

When their first son was born, a spirited someone threw a ghostly tantrum and dismantled the nursery the Roberts had prepared for their baby. Someone tore the bedclothes off and

Derek Roberts saw a ghostly guy standing at the foot of his bed, when Derek stirred, the apparition vanished.

Spirits calling the Roberts Ranch home dismantled this room twice to express their opinions of things.

scattered items throughout the room. The pictures were pulled off the walls. There was no one else in the house. Derek put everything back together again for the newborn's homecoming. When Derek, his wife and baby Burke arrived home from the hospital, they found the room totally dismantled again. Did it upset the resident ghosts to have a new baby living in their home?

Nancy Robinson, a local artist lived at the ranch house for a period to take care of things and keep everything in order. When she worked in the house, Nancy always felt that someone was approving of her cleaning the house but never saw anyone.

She confided her suspicions to a friend. The friend brought a psychic out to the house. The pair had told the psychic nothing. They were sitting and visiting while the psychic's two children were running wildly around the house.

The next day, Nancy's friend called to report what the psychic said. The friend asked the intuitive if she saw any ghosts and the psychic replied, "I saw a man and two women. All three of them were very worried that the kids might break some antiques!"

Nancy's son Forrest told of something he experienced at the ranch when he was six years old: He was playing in the ranch house with Ben Roberts and the boys were upstairs in Ben's room watching the Smurfs on TV. Forrest went downstairs to the kitchen for a snack. When he returned and walked upstairs, he saw an old man standing at the top of the steps. The man looked very tall to the little boy, but he didn't scare the youngster.

When the two passed on the steps, Forrest felt a chilling cold from him. As Forrest entered Ben's bedroom, the man disappeared. Forrest said the old man looked real. He refused to be frightened by what he saw until he was safely inside the bedroom and then he felt very scared. No one knew of an old man being in the house at the time.

Was he Uncle Ernie Roberts who had died some years before? The family thinks so.

Glen Haven

The tiny picture perfect village of Glen Haven is located seven miles north of Estes Park on Devil's Gulch Road.

The Inn

The Inn of Glen Haven is historic and exquisitely restored by Sheila and Tom Sellers. Enter into the comfortable, peaceful surroundings and you will think that any spirits lucky enough to live there must be very happy indeed.

Carol, a server for the Inn, told of a guest in the Lord Dunraven room who couldn't find her nightgown. The woman looked through everything in the room, looking for it. She

The happy spirits at the Glen Haven Inn appreciate the restoration and redecoration of the popular village establishment.

looked in all of the drawers, the closet and under the bed. Since she was packing to leave, she came downstairs and asked Carol to come up and help her. When the guest and Carol reached the room, they opened the door and saw the naughty nightgown laying flat on the bed waiting for its owner to retrieve it.

Sheila firmly believes the Inn is haunted. Her Cinderella story with the Inn began more than sixteen years ago. When she was married to her first husband, she and her children often drove to Estes Park for the weekend. They took the route from Drake through Glen Haven and once she spotted the Inn, she knew she had to have it. The Inn was always dark, dingy, and mysterious looking.

The abandoned and run down inn still appealed to the newly married bride. Sheila said that even though the building was filthy and in a shambles, she could feel the warmth of the building.

She said, "I thought even though everything is dirty and run down, and the reputation of the Inn is totally gone, the warmth of the building is intact and I can fix the rest".

Sheila and Tom applied for, and received a Small Business Administration Loan (SBA) within five weeks, unheard of in most cases. She said that everything went so smoothly, it was like there was a plan for them to own the Inn. Sheila has restored and decorated the Inn giving attention to every detail. Every change she has made, has worked out very well, she said.

When she was still working her day job for the phone company in Boulder, she drove home to Glen Haven at night to work more hours for the chef at the Inn. Sometimes, she stopped for a nap in Lyons because she was so exhausted. By the time, she reached the Inn all of her fatigue washed away. Her energy and enthusiasm is evident everywhere you look. The intimate old English décor feels completely blended into every inch of the building.

Sheila experienced her first spiritual encounter shortly after she and her husband bought the Inn. They were living in quarters upstairs.

The cantankerous chef for the Inn lived across the road with his three children. Everyone who worked at the Inn disliked him very much.

They hadn't owned the Inn very long. Sheila woke up one morning to the sound of children's footsteps running up and down the stairs. It was early and she was concerned the children running so noisily would disturb the guests. She waited for a little bit and all of a sudden, she heard children's voices singing *London Bridge*. Although Sheila is from England, she did not know the words to the famous song. She heard every word of the song very clearly in the children's voices that day, however.

Shortly after hearing the children sing, Sheila arose and dressed. She found the chef and proceeded to tell him that he shouldn't bring the children over to play in the Inn. Breakfast

Ghost children have been heard playing and singing on the stairway of the Inn. The cozy guest rooms keep the occupants oblivious to the spiritual antics in the hallways.

was served at eight, so most of the guests took advantage of the situation to catch up on some sleep.

Upon hearing this, the chef walked across the road to check on his kids. He returned, telling Sheila the children had not been in the Inn at all. They were still in their cabin, sleeping.

The singing voices were so clear to her. She could hear every word. She said she has never had a bad experience with the resident spirits. Sometimes, when she is upstairs ironing linens, she feels someone behind her, only no one is there.

One day, guests went hiking before leaving for home. One of them called Sheila the next day, to tell her they had forgotten some of their clothes and to ask her to send them. Sheila assured them she would but, when she entered the room to retrieve them, the clothes were missing. There was nothing in the drawers. She informed them she could not find their clothes.

She didn't think much about it after that, until she was cleaning the downstairs Charles Dickens Room. She opened the drawers to place fresh paper liner in them and found the missing clothes that had mysteriously moved from the room upstairs and made their way into a drawer in the Dickens Room downstairs. She packed them up and mailed the items to the guest, saying she felt like a "chump" because she didn't find the clothing earlier.

When you visit the romantic old Glen Haven Inn, maybe the spirits will communicate to you in some way.

Laporte

Laporte was Colona first, then La Porte and, in 1894, was designated Laporte. The town has been the site of the Overland Stage station, the Larimer county seat, and the original army camp before it moved to Fort Collins under the name of Camp Collins.

The Bingham Hill Cemetery

Located one half mile south of Laporte, Colorado. According to Rose Brink's book, History of the Bingham Hill Cemetery, "It is squeezed between an irrigation ditch and a field." There is a large black lettered sign with the name, Bingham Hill Cemetery. Many local residents did not know the cemetery existed until Rose began her work on it. There were no burials between 1942 and 1987. No one had to pay for burial space. No one kept burial records and no one is responsible for its care.

Enter Rose Brinks and fast forward to 2005. No one knows more about the Bingham Hill Cemetery than Rose Brink. She authored two books about it after she researched everyone interred there. She has also been the force behind the awareness of the cemetery. Many families are grateful to her for finding the resting places of their lost relatives. As for ghostly activity in the Bingham Hill Cemetery, she said she only knows of two incidents: We were unable to talk to the individual involved in the first paranormal incident.

The second one happened about three years ago, when there was a large gathering at the Brink's house. Rose led the guests over to the cemetery to reveal her adventures while researching the cemetery.

A Fort Collins man and his wife were among those enjoying the day, until, a woman dressed in a very fine leather dress, walked across an area in front of the man. He said that she had weathered skin as though she had spent a lot of time outdoors. He continued, "She walked very gracefully. The woman had dark hair pulled back and wore no jewelry. She was very slender." She appeared to be very real, and it was not until she suddenly disappeared into the air that he realized he had seen something out of the ordinary.

He admitted that he was not scared or threatened by her and did not say anything to the others who were standing nearby.

The Bingham Hill Cemetery is a quiet testimony to the proud heritage of Laporte.

He doesn't know if they saw her or not. He kept quiet and forgot about it until the next morning when he awoke suddenly and remembered what he witnessed the day before.

He and his wife revisited the Brink's home the next day to ask if anyone was assigned to walk around in costume to add a little flair to the program. Rose said no, that she hadn't arranged for anyone to do that. The man doesn't know what he saw, except that it was out of the ordinary. He will never forget the vanishing woman in the leather dress.

Rose asked in her book, "Who are the people under all the unmarked stones and the sunken places with no stones at all?"

Does the woman in the leather dress have any answers?

Glossary

apparition   A spirit visible to the human eye or captured on film. Can be in the form of an orb or ectoplasm.

ascension   To move on to the afterlife.

ectoplasm   The supposed emanation from the body of a medium.

ghost   A disembodied essence of someone who has been unable to ascend to the afterlife.

orb   A concentration of electro-magnetic energy, presumably from a spirit. It is visible as a solid white spot when captured on film.

poltergeist   A spirit manifesting itself by noises, knockings, etc.

spirit   A disembodied essence of someone who has unfinished business on the planet.

The Spirit or Spirit   God

Bibliography

Oral Histories

Business On Elkhorn, Museum Oral History Colorado 818. Estes Park Library. April 17, 1986.

Chansonetta Stanley Emmons, Library Oral History, Colorado 818. Estes Park Library, March 4, 1993.

Harold M. Dunning and Jack Moomaw, Library Oral History, Colorado 818, Estes Park Library, March 13, 1973.

Baldpate Inn (Mace Family), Library Oral History, Colorado 818, Estes Park Library, July 24, 1977.

Charles Eagle Plume, Library Oral History, Colorado 818, Estes Park Library, July 23, 1979.

Amazing Traveler Isabella Bird, By Evelyn Kaye, Blue Panda Publications, 1999.

Estes Park and Grand Lake By Caroline Bancroft, Johnson Publishing Co., 1968.

Estes Park From The Beginning By Dave Hicks, A-T-P Publishing, 1976.

Ghost Stories of the Estes Valley Vol. 1 By Celeste Lasky 0-9643331-3-9

Ghost Stories of the Estes Valley Vol. 2 By Celeste Lasky 0-9643331-4-7

Ghost Stories of the Rocky Mountains Vol. 2 By Barbara Smith 1-894877-21-7, 2003.

Historical Estes Park, Pictorial Edition, Estes Park Trail Gazette, 1968.

Bibliography

The Ways of The Mountains By James H. Pickering. Alpenaire Publishing, Inc. 2003.

Loveland's Historic Downtown-A Guide To Buildings, Loveland Museum Gallery, 2001.

Mariano Medina-The Colorado Mountain Man, By Zethyl Gates, Loveland Museum and Gallery, 1992.

Reflection on The River-The Big Thompson Canyon Flood, by Sharlynn Wamsley, Drake Club Press, 2001.

Thunder in The Rockies-The Incredible Denver Post, By Bill Hosokawa, William Morrow & Co., New York, 1976.

Index

G

H

I

J

About the Author

Nancy Hansford, the author of *Ghost Stories of Northern Colorado* is also the author of *Fort Collins Highlights*.

She loves living in Northern Colorado and telling the stories of those who are willing to share their experiences.

What is your story?

Dear Readers:

If you wish to share your personal ghost stories, e-mail your name, address, and phone number to: nanhansford@aol.com.

Nancy Hansford